JUMPIN' JIM'S
UKULELE TIPS 'N' TUNES
A Beginner's Method & Songbook
by Jim Beloff

Contents

Exclusively Distributed by
HAL LEONARD PUBLISHING CORPORATION
7777 West Bluemound Road
Milwaukee, Wisconsin 53213

Edited by Ronny S. Schiff
Graphic Design by Elyse Morris Wyman
Cover Illustration by Anita McLaughlin
Graphics and Charts by Charylu Roberts and Pete McDonnell

Foreword

Since the publication of my *Ukulele Favorites* songbook, I've heard from and met many ukulele fans. In fact, there are many more people playing the uke, collecting ukuleles and participating in ukulele clubs and groups than you might imagine. My own fascination with this instrument stems from the fact that it is extremely portable, and yet capable of producing remarkably sophisticated arrangements.

Somehow, once you get hooked on this "little guitar," you can't stop playing it and you can't stop encouraging others to play it too. *Tips 'N' Tunes* is my contribution. The challenge for me in writing this book was to give it some personality, make the learning process easy and fun, and, overall, try to create in print the experience of a private lesson.

One of the key innovations in this book is the use of "parenthetical" chords (⊞). This allows you to go back to a song that you've already learned and embellish it with more interesting chords.

I would love to hear from you. If you have any suggestions or anecdotes, please drop me a line.

—Jumpin' Jim

Also Available...

- **Jumpin' Jim's Ukulele Favorites**
  —A songbook featuring 30 great songs
  arranged for ukulele. $14.95
  (distributed by Hal Leonard Publishing Corp.)

- **Jim's Dog Has Fleas**
  —A CD of original songs for the uke by Jim Beloff.

  Visit us at www.fleamarketmusic.com

The Soprano Ukulele

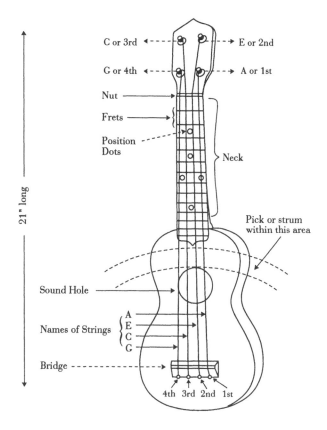

C or 3rd → E or 2nd
G or 4th → A or 1st
Nut
Frets
Position Dots
Neck
21" long
Pick or strum within this area
Sound Hole
Names of Strings { A E C G }
Bridge
4th 3rd 2nd 1st

The Family Of Ukuleles

Because the most common ukulele size is the soprano, this book has been written for the soprano ukulele (or any ukulele tuned GCEA). Ukes, however, come in many sizes. The baritone ukulele is usually tuned like the top four strings of a guitar (E B G D).

Soprano Concert Tenor Baritone

Holding The Uke

One of the best things about the uke is that it is so portable and light. Holding it while sitting or standing doesn't require a lot of effort. In fact, your best playing will come when you are the most relaxed.

Tips:

- Aim the neck at approximately 2:00 (see diagram above).

- Press the uke against you with the middle of your right forearm.

- Hold the neck between your thumb and first finger of your left hand, so that your fingers are free to move above the fingerboard.

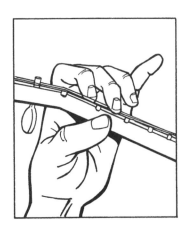
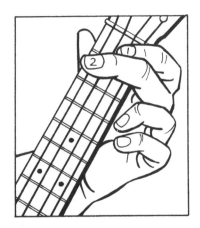

- With your right hand, strum the strings just above the sound hole (see above).

Tuning The Uke

Today, most soprano ukulele players use *C tuning*. In this tuning, the *open strings* (strings with no fingers on them) are named:

Uke C Tuning:

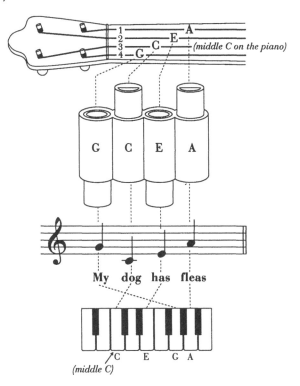

The easiest way to tune the ukulele is with a pitch pipe, matching the strings with the notes:

This corresponds to that famous melody:

Here are the notes on the keyboard:

(middle C)

Tuning Tips

How To Tune (with or without a pitchpipe or piano)...

1. Tune the first string to A (or high if you don't have anything to tune to).
2. On the second string E, place your finger on the fifth fret and tune the string so that it matches the sound of the first string.
3. On the third string C, place your finger on the fourth fret and tune the string to match the second string.
4. On the fourth string, place your finger on the second fret and match it to the first string.

You can also tune to the scale like this:

Tip—*Staying In Tune...*

On the back of each tuning peg you'll find a small screw. Keep this tight enough so that the pegs still turn, but your uke holds its tune.

Forming The Chords

Playing the ukulele requires two simultaneous actions: One is strumming the rhythm with your right hand. The second is forming the chords with your left hand.

In this book, you'll find diagrams (chord diagrams) that illustrate exactly what combination of open strings and fingered notes you should play to form each desired chord. They look like this:

These vertical lines indicate the strings:

G   C   E   A

4th   3rd   2nd   1st
string string string string

These horizontal lines indicate frets:

G   C   E   A

Nut
First fret
Second fret
Third fret

Dots on the chord diagrams indicate where to place your fingers.
The numbers at the bottom of the diagram indicate which finger to use:

1 = Index finger
2 = Second finger
3 = Ring finger
4 = Pinky
0 = Open string (no fingers)

Here are some sample chord diagrams:

C Chord

0   0   0   3

F Chord

2   0   1   0

G7 Chord

0   2   1   3

Front view

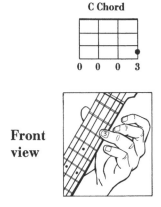

Tip—*Fingering Chords...*

- When pressing down the strings, use the tips of your fingers.
- Always press down in the space between the frets (not on them).
- Press the strings all the way down to the fingerboard.
- If you hear a buzz, you may not be pressing down hard enough or you may be too close to the fret.
- Keep your thumb at the back of the neck, parallel to the frets.

Chord Exercises

Moving quickly and gracefully from one chord to the next is essential to playing the uke. Practice the chords above in sequence. First practice fingering and playing each chord several times by brushing your thumb down across the strings. Then slowly switch back and forth between chords and increase your speed until you can move fluidly between them.

Strumming The Strings

Most ukulele players use their thumb and fingers to create the strums. This gives them the most rhythmic options.

Try strumming with just your thumb…

Or index finger:

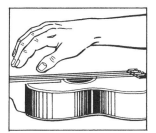

You may wish to start out with a pick. The ukulele pick is made of felt and produces a soft, brushed tone.

Hold the pick lightly between your thumb and first finger with the smaller end pointing out:

The best way to move the pick across the strings is in a smooth, even downward motion. Try this:

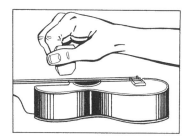

Remember to keep the movement exclusively in your hand and not in your forearm.

Symbols For Strums…

⊓ **Downstroke** – movement is downward, or away from you.

V **Upstroke** – movement is upward, or toward you.

Exercise…

Now try the following chords with all downstrokes and then all upstrokes. Practice in groups of 4 strokes per chord. Repeat until your strum is smooth and even, and the chords sound clear.

C Chord	F Chord	G7 Chord	C Chord
0 0 0 3	2 0 1 0	0 2 1 3	0 0 0 3

Tip—You may find that your thumb works better on downstrokes, while your index finger can be used for both up- and downstrokes. A pick will work fine in both directions.

7

Reading The Music

Here are the most basic principles of music. Understanding these fundamentals will ultimately make the process of learning the ukulele (or any musical instrument) easier and more interesting.

The melodies of the songs in this book are written on a musical *staff*. This staff, consisting of five lines and four spaces, is where the notes are placed. The notes indicate both pitch and duration.

a staff

The Treble Clef

Ukulele music is always written in the *treble clef* (𝄞). The treble or G clef, which is always placed at the beginning of each song, establishes the position of the note G on the second line of the staff. Then, from it you can determine where all the other notes are positioned.

G

The Full Scale

The first seven letters of the alphabet are used for naming the lines and spaces. After the seven letters are named, they repeat themselves...*

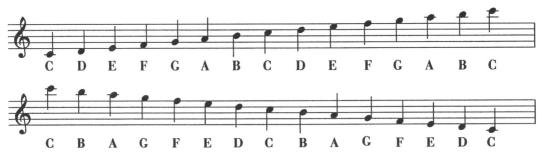

C D E F G A B C D E F G A B C

C B A G F E D C B A G F E D C

See page 62 for a fretboard diagram and the corresponding notes on each string.

Tip —Here are some tricks to remember the notes in the lines and the notes in the spaces...

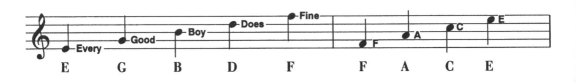

Every — Good — Boy — Does — Fine

E G B D F   F A C E

Measures and Bar Lines

The staff is divided into equal parts called *measures*. The measures are divided by bar lines:

Two twin double bars are placed at the end of a verse or chorus.

One thin and one thick double bar indicate the end of a song.

These symbols indicate to repeat all the measures in between them.

Note Values and Rest Durations

The shape of each note and each rest determines the length of time each is to be held. A *rest* indicates a period of silence.

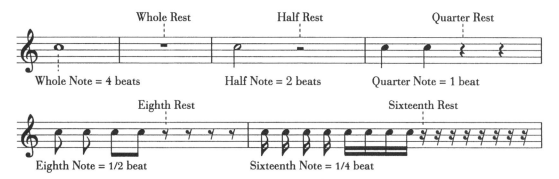

Whole Rest   Half Rest   Quarter Rest

Whole Note = 4 beats   Half Note = 2 beats   Quarter Note = 1 beat

Eighth Rest   Sixteenth Rest

Eighth Note = 1/2 beat   Sixteenth Note = 1/4 beat

Whenever a dot appears after a note, it increases the note's duration by one half, for instance:

Dotted Half Note: 𝅗𝅥. = 𝅗𝅥 + ♩   3 beats

Dotted Quarter Note: ♩. = ♩ + ♪   1 1/2 beats

Dotted Eighth Note: ♪. = ♪ + ♪   3/4 beat

Time Signatures

At the beginning of each song, you will find a *time signature*. These numbers tell you:

4 ← How many beats are in a measure *(four)*
4 ← The type of note receiving that beat *(a quarter note)*

This 4 means that there are four beats to this measure →
This 4 means that each quarter note equals one beat →

4 quarter notes, 2 half notes, 1 whole note

This 2 means that there are two beats to this measure →
This 4 means that each quarter note equals one beat →

2 quarter notes,   1 half note

This 3 means that there are three beats to this measure →
This 4 means that each quarter note equals one beat →

3 quarter notes,   1 dotted half note

Sharps and Flats & Key Signatures

Sharps And Flats

The sharp symbol (♯), the flat symbol (♭) and the natural symbol (♮) all affect and change the notes they precede...

Sharp ♯   Raises a note one fret (musically, one half-step higher)

Flat ♭   Lowers a note one fret (musically, one half-step lower)

Natural ♮   Restores the note to its original (starting) tone, therefore cancelling out a sharp or flat

Key Signature Table

The songs in this book are divided into groups by keys. The sharps (♯) and the flats (♭) shown at the beginning of each song apply to all notes of the same name throughout the song. As you can see, C major has no sharps of flats.

Major Keys		Relative Minor Keys	Major Keys		Relative Minor Keys
C Major		A minor	C Major		A minor
G Major		E minor	F Major		D minor
D Major		B minor	B♭ Major		G minor
A Major		F♯ minor	E♭ Major		C minor
E Major		C♯ minor	A♭ Major		F minor
B Major		G♯ minor	D♭ Major		B♭ minor
F♯ Major		D♯ minor	G♭ Major		E♭ minor
C♯ Major		A♯ minor	C♭ Major		A♭ minor

Songs In the Key of C

He's Got The Whole World In His Hands

Considering that the ukulele, in my opinion, is such a swell instrument, it seems wholly appropriate that your first uke song is "He's Got The Whole World In His Hands." Just two chords, a simple downstroke strum and you're playing your first tune. The "first note" indicates your first singing note (in this case, the open G string).

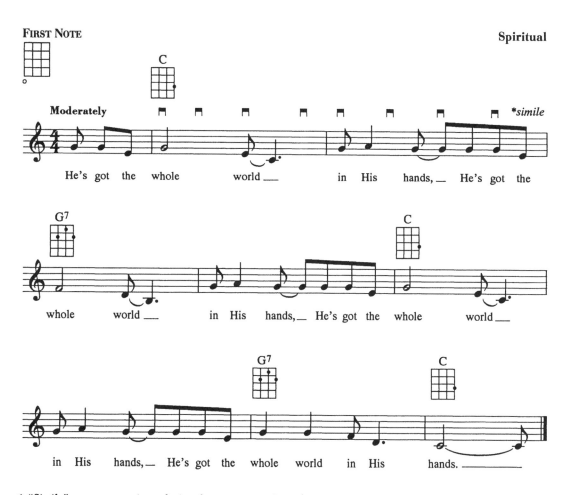

* *"Simile"* means to continue playing the same strum throughout

Alternate Strum

Clementine

Your first song in 3/4 time…While this song can be played with two chords and a downward strum, don't hesitate to return later and try the alternative strum and the parenthetical chords. As I mentioned earlier, these chords add flavor to the arrangement. Start by adding the easiest ones to play and add more as you gain confidence.

Late 19th Century Folk Song

In a cav-ern, in a can-yon ex-ca-va-ting for a mine, dwelt a

min-er, 'for-ty-nin-er and his daugh-ter, Clem-en-tine.   Oh, my

darl-ing, oh, my darl-ing, oh, my darl-ing, Clem-en-tine,   you are

lost and gone for-ev-er, dread-ful sor-ry, Clem-en-tine.

Alternate Strum

Buffalo Gals

Your third song has the same two chords as the first two, but introduces a fast up/down strum *(Common Strum)*. Note that the chorus features a rhythmic "hiccup" (a missing downstroke) that adds more variety to the arrangement. Once you've mastered this, look for other places in the upcoming songs to put in these kind of rhythmic breaks.

The Common Strum—This strum is the foundation for all the strums. It is produced with the first or index finger, or the thumb and index finger.

With your index finger, you strike downward with your fingernail and up with the cushion of your fingertip (see diagrams below). You can also try this with your thumb going down and the tip of your index finger going up.

While your wrist and finger must be flexible for good tone, do not allow your wrist to move up and down.

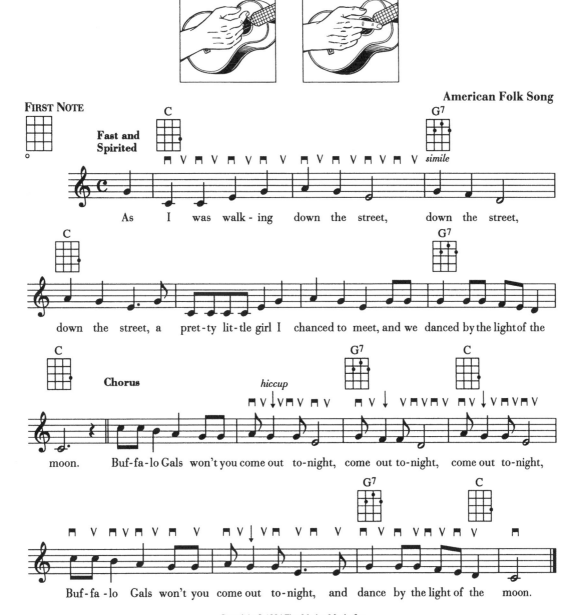

As I was walk-ing down the street, down the street, down the street, a pret-ty lit-tle girl I chanced to meet, and we danced by the light of the moon. Buf-fa-lo Gals won't you come out to-night, come out to-night, come out to-night, Buf-fa-lo Gals won't you come out to-night, and dance by the light of the moon.

American Folk Song

Amazing Grace

F
2010

Say "hello" to the F chord; after G7 it's the next most important chord in the key of C. Note, too, how adding the C7 gives the arrangement more tonal feeling. Don't forget to try the alternative strum.

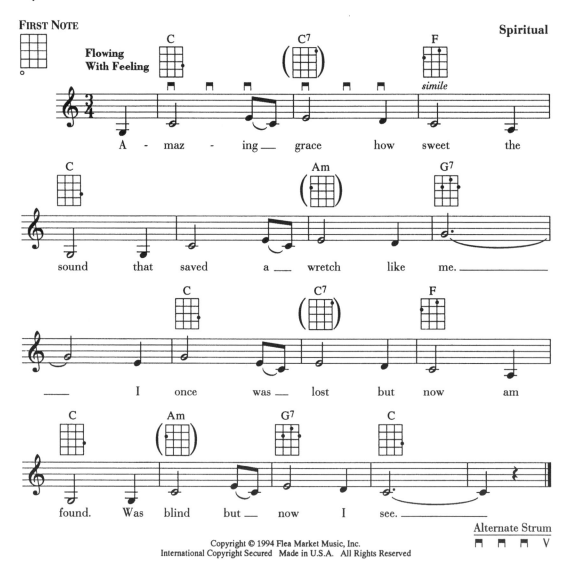

Did you know...

The Tsumura Collection

Akira Tsumura, a successful Japanese businessman, is considered by many experts to have the world's greatest collection of vintage ukuleles. This is in addition to his world's greatest collection of banjos and guitars! Mr. Tsumura began collecting banjos in 1963; it was around that time that he also became interested in ukes and aware of the need to preserve them. Currently, the Tsumura Collection includes 400 ukuleles, many of which can be seen in a book he published called *Guitars—The Tsumura Collection*.

When The Saints Go Marching In

This song features a new popular strum. In fact, you'll find many examples of it in this book. Just remember that the downstrokes occur on the downbeats. In this case, the upstrokes only occur on the "and" of the second and third beats.

P.S. Doesn't that F minor chord sound great?

The Climbing Song

G#7

Here's an "original." Actually it's a little ditty I came up with while hiking in Maine. It introduces a chord, G#7, that's not found in the key of C.

FIRST NOTE

Words and Music by
Jim Beloff

Songs In The Key Of G

She'll Be Comin' 'Round The Mountain

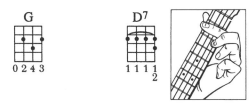

The key of G has one sharp in it—F#. Two of the most important chords in the key of G are C and D7. The D7 is an example of a barred chord. To form the chord, lay your first finger across the entire second fret, keeping it as straight as possible. If there are no buzzes, then put your second finger on the third fret of the first string. Now you've formed a D7.

The Band Played On

A new 3/4 strum. There are a couple of ways to play a C6 (the sixth measure) on the uke. One easy way is to simply strum the four open strings without any fingers on the fretboard.

Words by John E. Palmer
Music by Charles B. Ward

Cas - ey would waltz with a straw - ber - ry blonde and the

band played on. _____ He'd

glide 'cross the floor with the girl he a - dored, and the

band played on. _____ But his

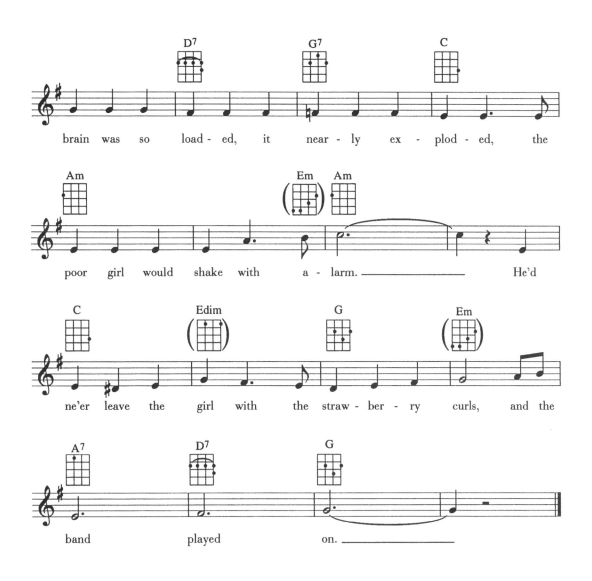

brain was so load - ed, it near - ly ex - plod - ed, the

poor girl would shake with a - larm. _____ He'd

ne'er leave the girl with the straw - ber - ry curls, and the

band played on. _____

A bevy of banjo ukes, 1994.
Photo by Elizabeth Maihock Beloff.

19

Aura Lee

Cmaj7   0 0 0 3

E7   1 2 0 3

Note that in the fourth to the last measure, the E7 hits on the third beat. This tune should sound familiar; it's the melody for Elvis Presley's "Love Me Tender."

Words by W.W. Fosdick
Music by George R. Poulton

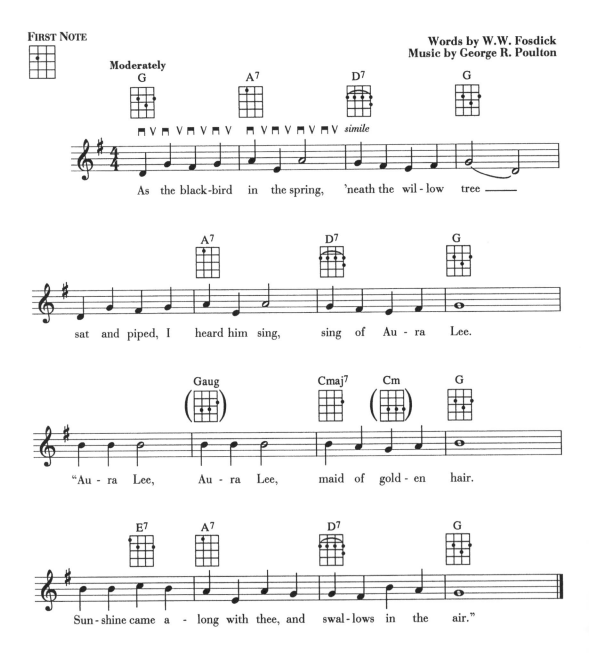

As the black-bird in the spring, 'neath the wil-low tree _____

sat and piped, I heard him sing, sing of Au - ra Lee.

"Au - ra Lee, Au - ra Lee, maid of gold - en hair.

Sun - shine came a - long with thee, and swal - lows in the air."

Bill Bailey, Won't You Please Come Home

The strums in this book are very basic. Once you've learned the chords to "Bill Bailey," try some variations on the strums (especially around the optional quick change from Gdim to G where you can use one downstroke instead of what's written).

Words and Music by
Hughie Cannon

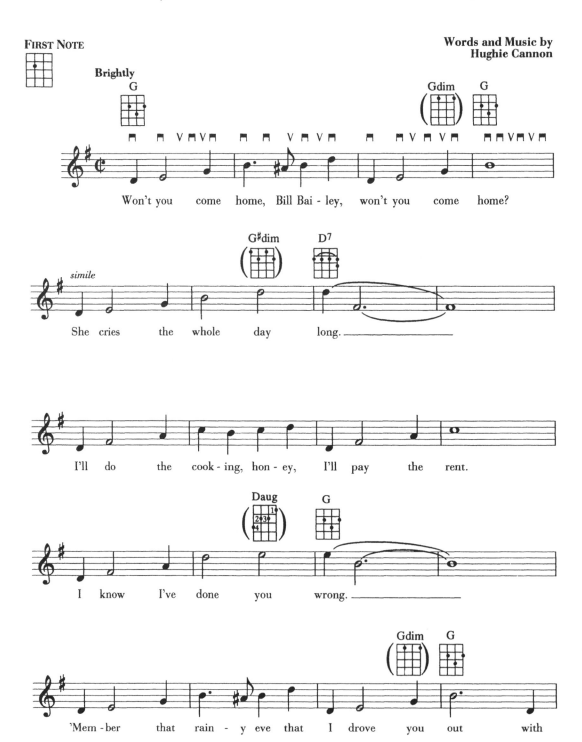

Won't you come home, Bill Bai - ley, won't you come home?

She cries the whole day long. ____

I'll do the cook - ing, hon - ey, I'll pay the rent.

I know I've done you wrong. ____

'Mem - ber that rain - y eve that I drove you out with

noth-in' but a fine-tooth comb? _____ I

know I'm to blame, well, ain't that a shame? Bill

Bai-ley won't you please come home? _____

The Uke On Record

There have been a number of very good recordings featuring the ukulele. Some are easier to find than others, since, unfortunately, many are vintage recordings and have not been re-released (yet). Ohta-San, one of the finest ukulele players alive today, continues to live and play in Hawaii, as well as record periodically. All of his recordings are recommended. So are any of the uke recordings of Cliff Edwards (Ukulele Ike—see *Jumpin' Jim's Ukulele Favorites*) and Roy Smeck. You'll find plenty of uke strumming on Ian Whitcomb's recordings, all of which are currently available. One of my favorite recordings is *How About Uke?*, a jazz ukulele recording by Lyle Ritz put out by Verve records in the 1950s.

Roy Smeck, known as "The Wizard Of The Strings," one of the greatest uke players of all time. He also lent his name to a number of ukes made by the Harmony company of Chicago.

Three Harmony ukuleles; left and right are the Smeck signature ukes.
Photo by Elizabeth Maihock Beloff

You Tell Me Your Dream

Like "Bill Bailey," this song contains a measure with two chords in it (the second to the last measure). Learning to move quickly from one chord to another in two beats (or less) is critical to becoming an accomplished uke player. Start out just going back and forth between the chords until you can change from one to the other in tempo.

Words by Albert Brown and
Seymour Rice
Music by Charles N. Daniels

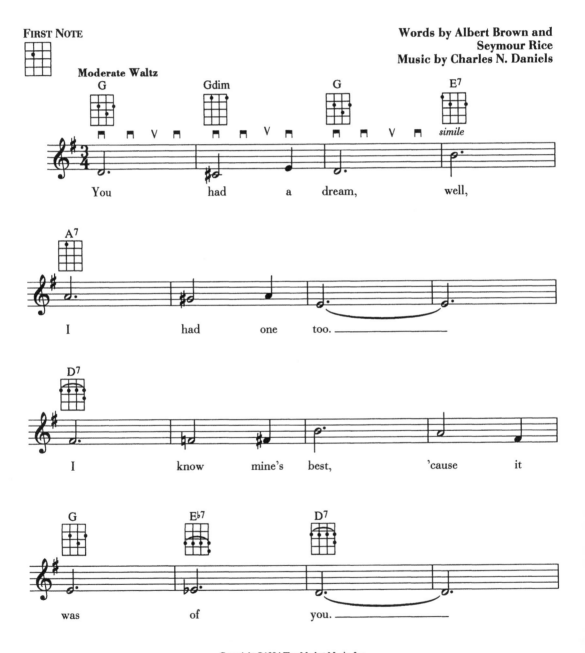

G   Gdim   G E^7

Come,   sweet - heart,   tell   me,

A^7

now   is   the   time. _____

C   Gdim   G E^7

You   tell   me   your   dream,

A^7 D^7 G   Gdim   G

I'll   tell   you   mine. _____

Ian Whitcomb, British pop star turned ukester, is busy keeping old standards alive.

The Sidewalks Of New York

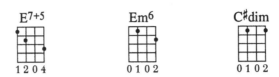

The up/down stroke on the third beat gives this arrangement a little lift. Also featured are really interesting chord changes like the E7+5 to E7, the Em6 and C#dim.

Words by James W. Blake
Music by Charles B. Lawlor

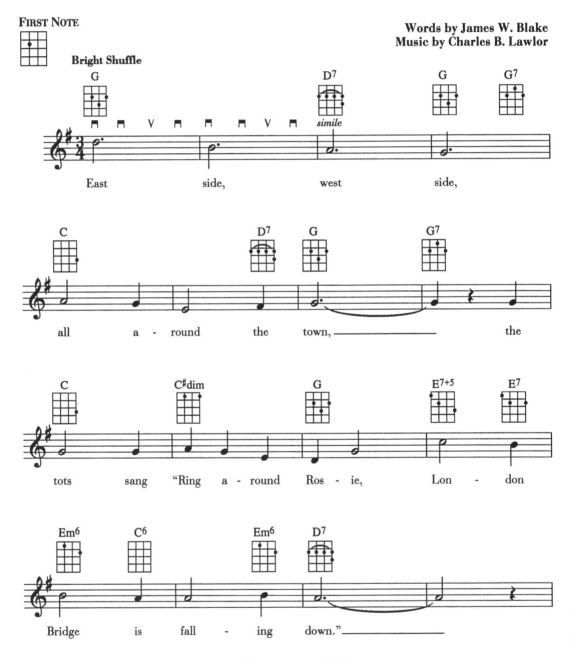

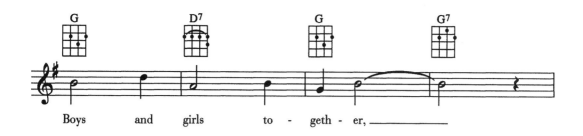

Boys   and   girls   to - geth - er, _____

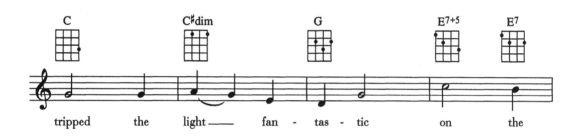

me   and   Ma - mie O' Rourke _____

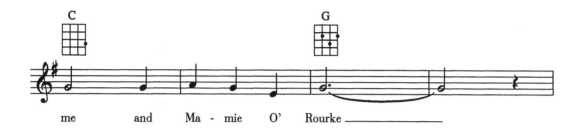

tripped   the   light ____ fan - tas - tic   on   the

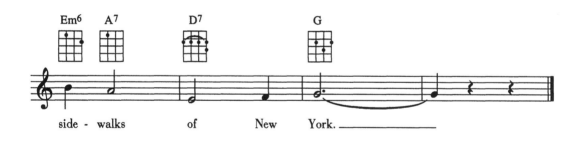

side - walks   of   New   York. _____

I've Been Working On The Railroad

Here's a new strum. Don't let the additional B7sus to B7 scare you. All it means is moving one finger back one fret—and, oh, do they add to the arrangement!

The Konter Ukulele

The first instrument to cross the North Pole was a plain koa wood Martin ukulele owned by Richard Wesley Konter. An American seaman and adventurer, Konter was a volunteer on Commander Byrd's first expedition over the North Pole on May 9, 1926. With the help of the pilot, Konter smuggled the ukulele aboard. This uke was later given to the Martin Company by Konter, and can be seen in the Martin Museum in Nazareth, Pennsylvania.

Front view

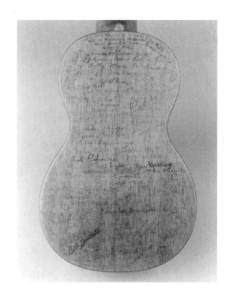

Back view

Note the signatures of members of the Byrd expedition party.

Information courtesy of Mike Longworth from his Martin Guitars—A History, *1988. Photo courtesy of the Martin Guitar Company.*

Songs In The Key Of F

A Bicycle Built For Two (Daisy Bell)

Two of the most popular chords in the key of F are B♭ and C7. B♭ (like F on the guitar) is one of the more difficult chords to play. The good news is once you can play it without any "buzzing strings," everything else is a piece of cake.

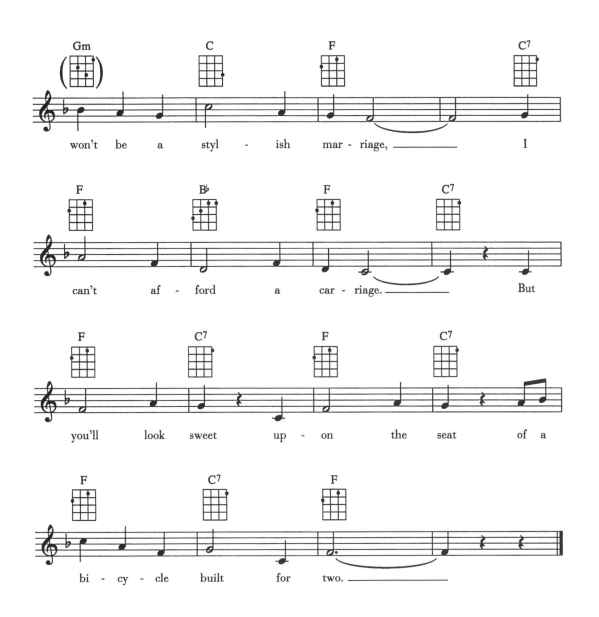

won't be a styl - ish mar - riage, _____ I
can't af - ford a car - riage. _____ But
you'll look sweet up - on the seat of a
bi - cy - cle built for two. _____

Ukulele Ike
Photo courtesy of Ian Whitcomb / ITW Industries © 1992

Oh, Susanna

Here's a new strum. Just a reminder to initially play these songs at a slower tempo to get the hang of the chord changes. Once you can play them at tempo, then dazzle your friends.

Words and Music by
Stephen Foster

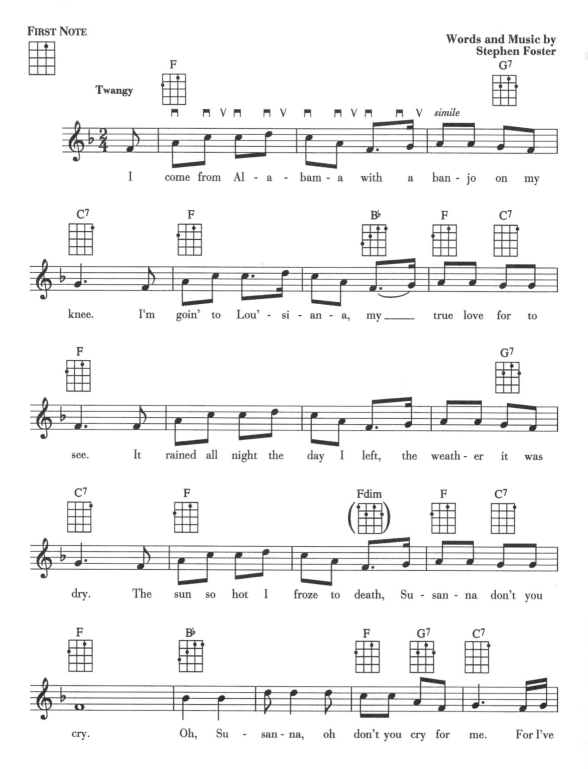

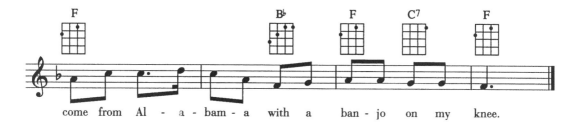

come from Al - a - bam - a with a ban - jo on my knee.

America

Like all good things, this arrangement takes time to master. But it is the closest arrangement so far to "chord soloing." "Chord soloing" means that your melody notes are found within the chord progressions—which means you are playing melody with an accompaniment simultaneously. Also, note the altered F chord in the seventh measure: This variation puts the high C in the chord, which is also in the melody.

FIRST NOTE

Slowly and Proudly

Words by Samuel Francis Smith
Music based on "God Save the Queen"

My coun - try, 'tis of thee, sweet land of lib - er - ty of thee I sing. Land where my fa - thers died, land of the Pil - grim's pride, from ev' - ry — moun - tain - side let — free - dom ring!

Home On The Range

All chord fingerings are based on years of experience. Nonetheless, you may find more comfortable finger placement. If so, go with your instincts.

Attributed to:
Words by Brewster Higley
Music by Daniel E. Kelly

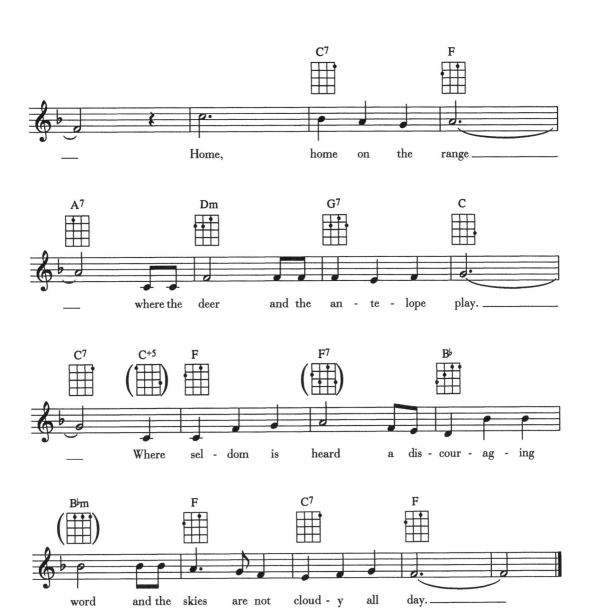

You're A Grand Old Flag

This arrangement features rhythm marks throughout. Take your time with it and feel free to add your own strum embellishments.

Words and Music by
George M. Cohan

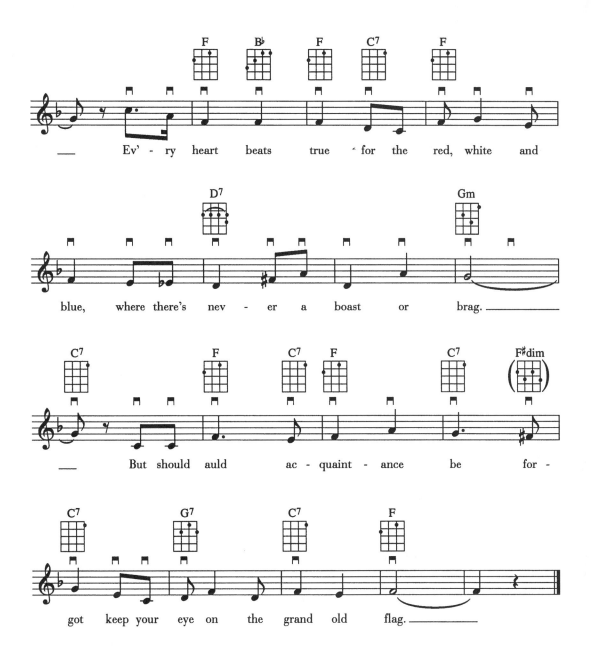

Ev' - ry heart beats true for the red, white and

blue, where there's nev - er a boast or brag. _____

_____ But should auld ac - quaint - ance be for -

got keep your eye on the grand old flag. _____

Swing Low, Sweet Chariot

F7
2 3 1 4

Another arrangement including more than one strum! For added drama, try adding a roll strum or tremolo at the end of the song (see below). "D.C. al Fine" means "return to the beginning and play to the word *fine.*"

The Roll Strum—The roll strum is produced in the same manner as the common strum, but with the fingers stroking the strings one after the other quickly, giving them the effect of a rolling drum.

Start the strum with the nail of your little finger, followed by your third, second and first fingers.

Try for a smooth, continuous roll. Don't move too fast, but surely and evenly.

The Tremolo—This strum is essentially the common strum, but it is played up and down quickly, creating a tremolo or "organ" effect. It's especially useful to add expression and drama.

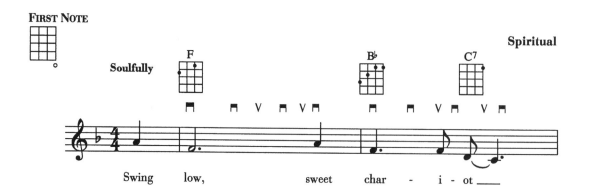

Songs In The Key Of B♭

While Strolling Through The Park One Day

Two of the most important chords in the key of B♭ are F7 and E♭.

course, we were as hap-py as can be. Ah! I im-me-di-ate-ly raised my hat, and fin-al-ly she re-marked... I nev-er shall for-get, that love-ly af-ter-noon, I met her at the foun-tain in the park.

⌢ = *hold the note longer*

Did you know...

The Uke And Hollywood

The ukulele has been featured in some pretty noteworthy movies. Perhaps the uke's biggest role was as the instrument of Marilyn Monroe in *Some Like It Hot*. You'll also find Elvis Presley strumming a ukulele in *Blue Hawaii*. Of course, the uke has been seen on television thanks to the performances of Arthur Godfrey, Tiny Tim, Roy Smeck and Lawrence Welk.

Tiny Tim
Photo courtesy of Archive Photos, New York

Give My Regards To Broadway

Cm⁷

Doesn't that alternate chord, Faug, sound great?

Words and Music by
George M. Cohan

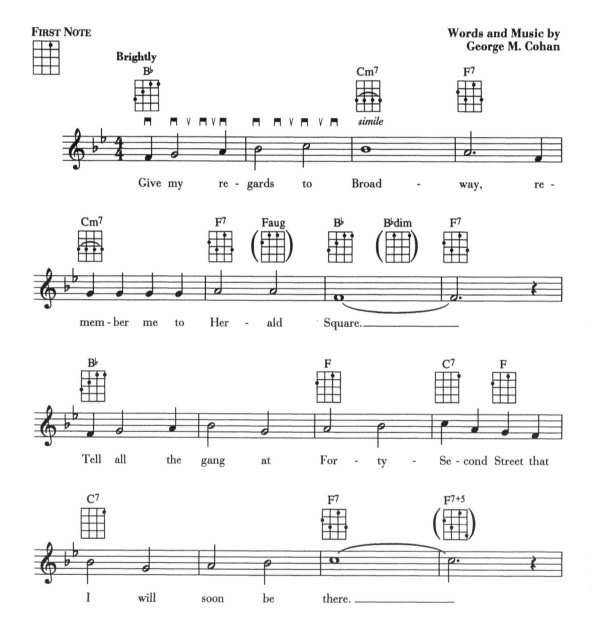

Give my re-gards to Broad - way, re-mem-ber me to Her - ald Square. Tell all the gang at For - ty - Se-cond Street that I will soon be there.

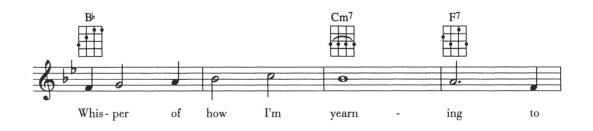

Whis - per of how I'm yearn - ing to

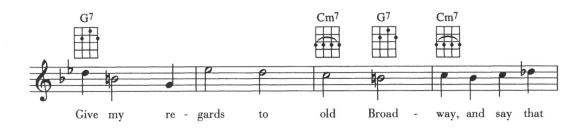

min - gle with the old - time throng. _____

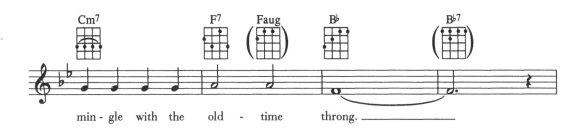

Give my re - gards to old Broad - way, and say that

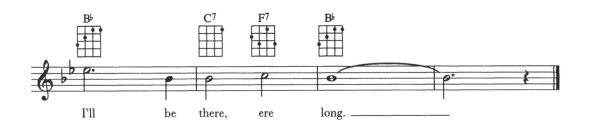

I'll be there, ere long. _____

Let Me Call You Sweetheart

I've often thought that good uke arranging is like barbershop singing. This song is a good example of that, especially in the *"I'm in love with you..."* chords.

Keep the love - light glow - ing in your

eyes so true. _____

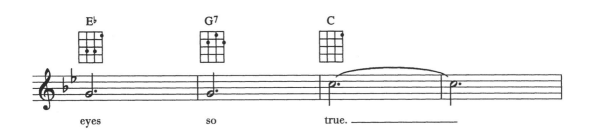

Let me call you sweet - heart, I'm in

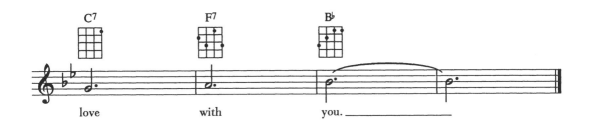

love with you. _____

45

The Star Spangled Banner

Play this standing up. Actually, play this and the next two songs standing up. B♭ must be the patriotic key!

Words by Francis Scott Key
Music by John Stafford Smith

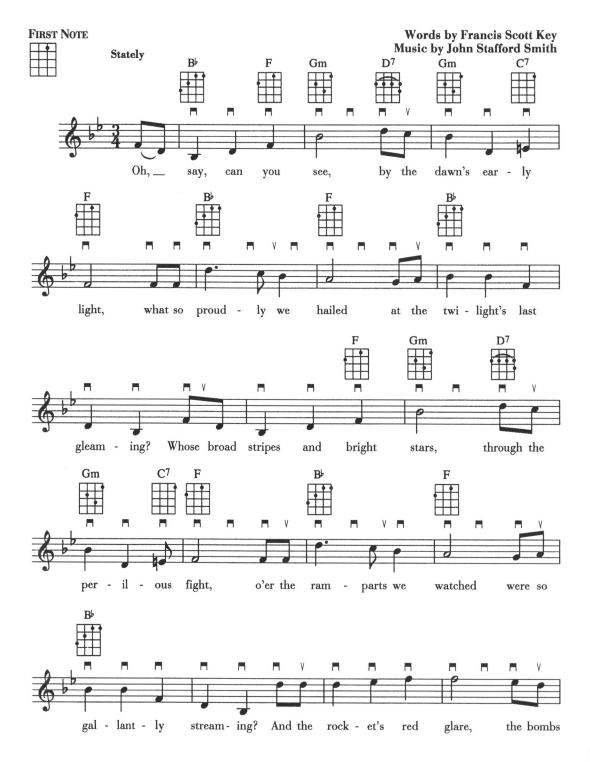

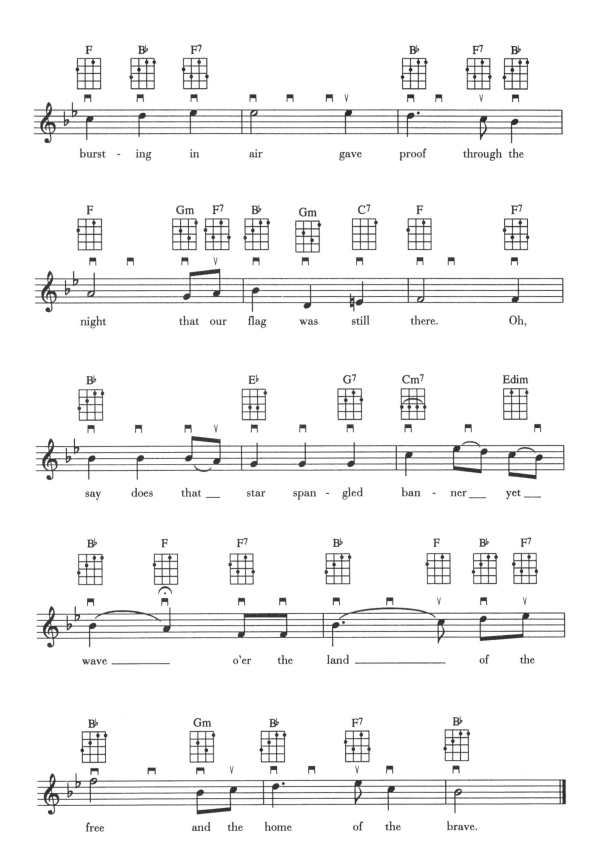

Yankee Doodle Boy

Work hard at making the succession of changes from F7 to B♭ (in the last eight measures) as clean and clear as possible.

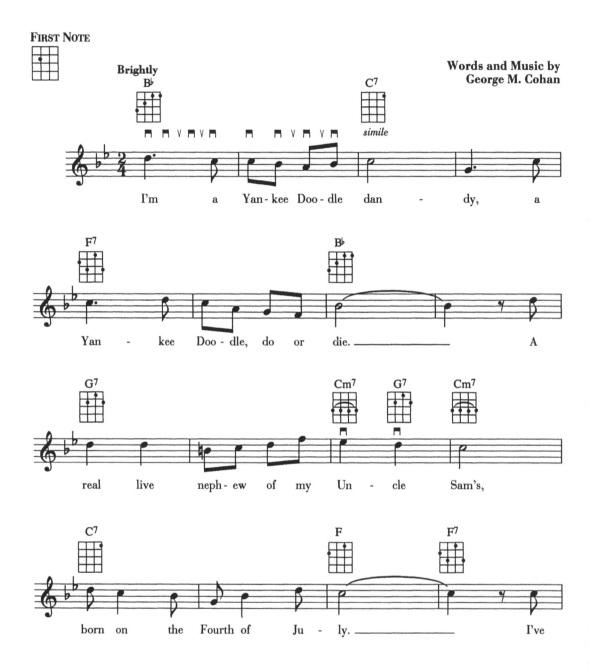

Words and Music by
George M. Cohan

I'm a Yan-kee Doo-dle dan - dy, a

Yan - kee Doo-dle, do or die. _____ A

real live neph-ew of my Un - cle Sam's,

born on the Fourth of Ju - ly. _____ I've

got   a   Yan - kee Doo - dle   sweet   -   heart

she's   my   Yan - kee Doo - dle   joy. _____

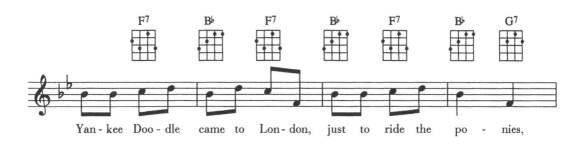

Yan - kee Doo - dle came to Lon - don, just to ride the   po — nies,

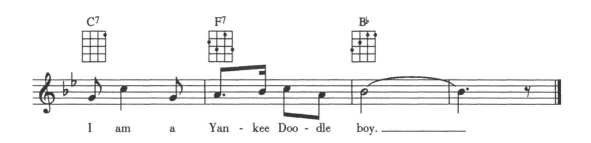

I am   a   Yan - kee Doo - dle boy. _____

America, The Beautiful

Watch the alternating rhythm and strums.

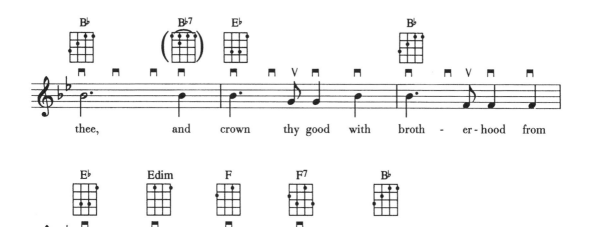

thee,   and   crown   thy good   with   broth - er - hood   from

sea   to   shin - ing   sea.

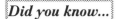

The Maccaferri Ukulele

Mario Maccaferri (1900-1993) was the developer of the first and most popular plastic ukulele. Maccaferri—a well-known performer, inventor and guitar maker (the Maccaferri-Selmer guitar was popularized by the renowned Django Reinhardt)—became fascinated with the potential of plastics in the late '40s. In 1950, he combined his knowledge of guitar making and plastics to create the "Islander" uke. After getting the endorsement of Arthur Godfrey, sales took off. At a retail price of $4.95, over 9 million of his ukes were sold between 1950 and 1958.

The famous $4.95 Maccaferri uke
Photo by Elizabeth Maihock Beloff

Arthur Godfrey
Photo courtesy of Archive Photos, New York

Songs In The Key Of D

Beautiful Dreamer

D · Em · D9

2 3 4 0 · 3 4 2 1 · 1 3 1 2

Two of the most important chords in the key of D are G and A7.

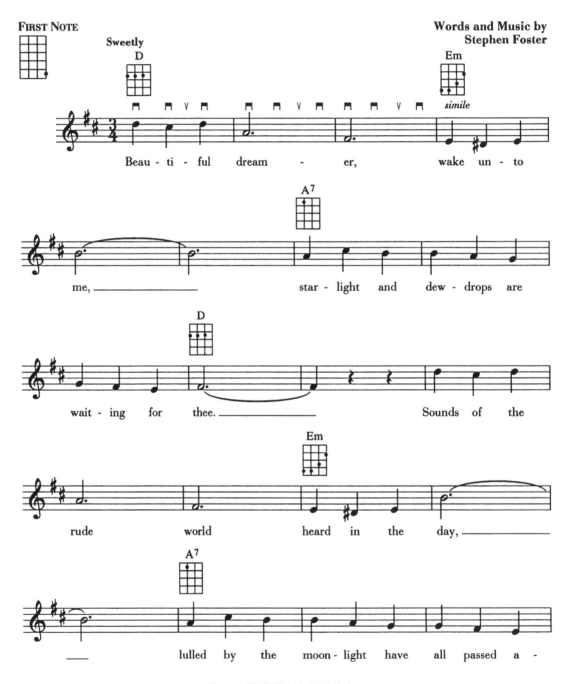

FIRST NOTE

Sweetly

Words and Music by
Stephen Foster

Beau - ti - ful dream - er, wake un - to
me, _____ star - light and dew - drops are
wait - ing for thee. _____ Sounds of the
rude world heard in the day, _____
_ lulled by the moon - light have all passed a -

Drink To Me Only With Thine Eyes

A very simple melody with a lot of chord changes occurring on every beat.

Words by Ben Johnson
Music: Old English Air

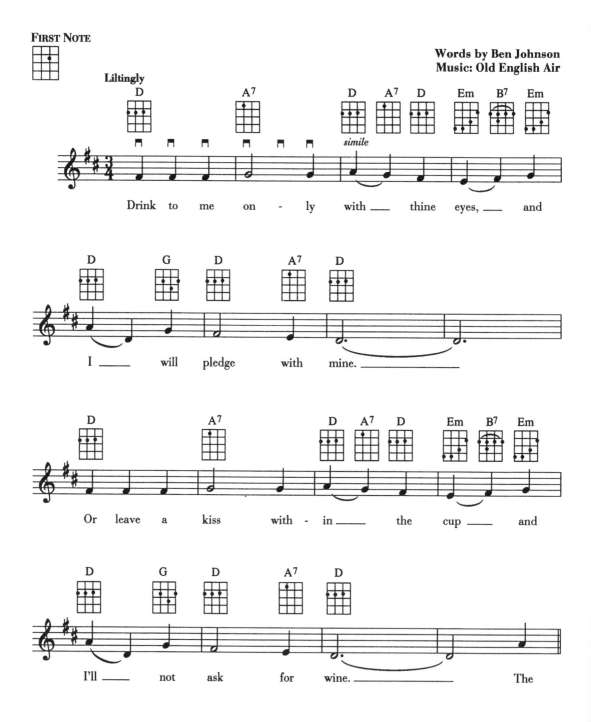

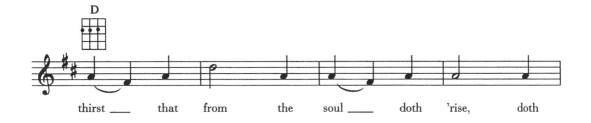

thirst ___ that from the soul ___ doth 'rise, doth

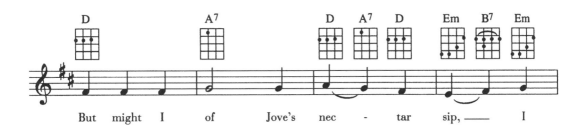

ask a drink ___ di - vine. _____

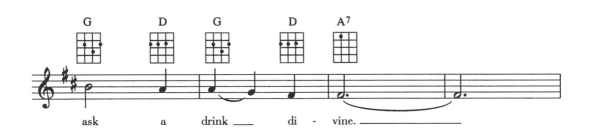

But might I of Jove's nec - tar sip, ___ I

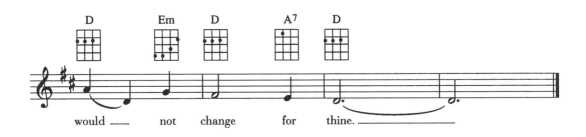

would ___ not change for thine. _____

55

Song In The Key Of A♭

Aloha Oe

This classic Hawaiian song is in an unusual key. It's a challenge to you, so you can practice playing with all barred chords.

Three Hawaiian ukes—Kamaka, Bergstrom, L. Nuñez
Photo by Elizabeth Maihock Beloff

Hawaiian girl, Kohala Seminary, 1915
R.J. Baker Collection, Bishop Museum,
Honolulu, Hawaii

Maria Lane and friend with ukuleles,
1886 A.F. Mitchell, Bishop Museum,
Honolulu, Hawaii

Samuel K. Kamaka holding his pineapple ukulele.
Photo courtesy of Kamaka Hawaii, Inc.

Song In All Keys

The Key Change Song

If you've gotten to this point, and you can play this song, then give yourself a round of applause. The "Key Change Song" is just that—a practice tune that takes you through all the major chords.

FIRST NOTE

Music and Lyrics by
Jim Beloff

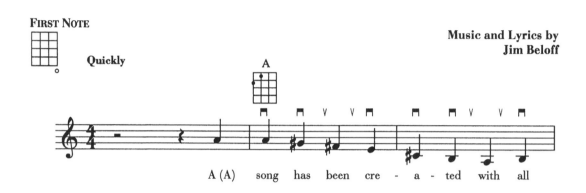

A (A) song has been cre - a - ted with all

ma - jor chords.— A song that fea - tures

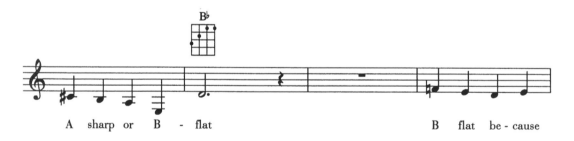

A sharp or B - flat B flat be - cause

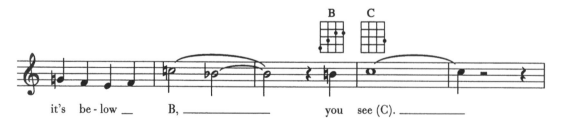

it's be - low __ B, _____ you see (C). _____

C sharp fol - lows   C   un - less   it's   D ____ flat. ____

____   D   flat   is   a   half step down from   D. ____

____   D sharp or   E   flat is com - ing   next, ____

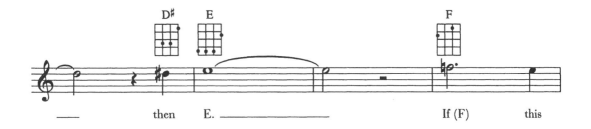

____   then   E. ____   If (F)   this

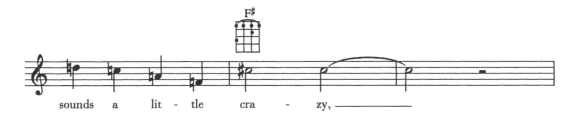

sounds   a   lit - tle   cra - zy, ____

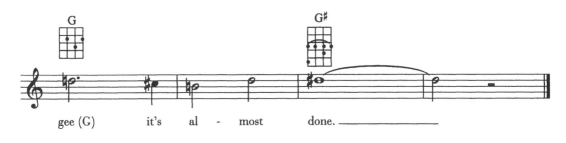

gee (G)   it's   al - most   done. ____

Chord Chart

MAJOR CHORDS

A A#/Bb B C C#/Db D D#/Eb E F F#/Gb G G#/Ab

MINOR CHORDS

Am A#m/Bbm Bm Cm C#m/Dbm Dm D#m/Ebm Em Fm F#m/Gbm Gm G#m/Abm

DOMINANT SEVENTH CHORDS

A7 A#7/Bb7 B7 C7 C#7/Db7 D7 D#7/Eb7 E7 F7 F#7/Gb7 G7 G#7/Ab7

DOMINANT NINTH CHORDS

A9 A#9/Bb9 B9 C9 C#9/Db9 D9 D#9/Eb9 E9 F9 F#9/Gb9 G9 G#9/Ab9

MINOR SEVENTH CHORDS

Am7 A#m7/Bbm7 Bm7 Cm7 C#m7/Dbm7 Dm7 D#m7/Ebm7 Em7 Fm7 F#m7/Gbm7 Gm7 G#m7/Abm7

MAJOR SIXTH CHORDS

A6 A#6/Bb6 B6 C6 C#6/Db6 D6 D#6/Eb6 E6 F6 F#6/Gb6 G6 G#6/Ab6

MINOR SIXTH CHORDS

Am6 | A#m6 B♭m6 | Bm6 | Cm6 | D♭m6 C#m6 | Dm6 | D#m6 E♭m6 | Em6 | Fm6 | G♭m6 F#m6 | Gm6 | A♭m6 G#m6

MAJOR SEVENTH CHORDS

Amaj7 | A#maj7 B♭maj7 | Bmaj7 | Cmaj7 | D♭maj7 C#maj7 | Dmaj7 | D#maj7 E♭maj7 | Emaj7 | Fmaj7 | G♭maj7 F#maj7 | Gmaj7 | A♭maj7 G#maj7

DOMINANT SEVENTH CHORDS WITH RAISED FIFTH (7th+5)

A7+5 | A#7+5 B♭7+5 | B7+5 | C7+5 | D♭7+5 C#7+5 | D7+5 | D#7+5 E♭7+5 | E7+5 | F7+5 | G♭7+5 F#7+5 | G7+5 | A♭7+5 G#7+5

DOMINANT SEVENTH CHORDS WITH LOWERED FIFTH (7th-5)

A7-5 | A#7-5 B♭7-5 | B7-5 | C7-5 | D♭7-5 C#7-5 | D7-5 | D#7-5 E♭7-5 | E7-5 | F7-5 | G♭7-5 F#7-5 | G7-5 | A♭7-5 G#7-5

AUGMENTED FIFTH CHORDS (AUG. or +)

Aaug | A#aug B♭aug | Baug | Caug | D♭aug C#aug | Daug | D#aug E♭aug | Eaug | Faug | G♭aug F#aug | Gaug | A♭aug G#aug

DIMINISHED SEVENTH CHORDS (Dim.)

Adim | A#dim B♭dim | Bdim | Cdim | D♭dim C#dim | Ddim | D#dim E♭dim | Edim | Fdim | G♭dim F#dim | Gdim | A♭dim G#dim

Transposing

When you want to change the key of a song (for instance if it's too high or low to sing), it is necessary to change all of the chords. In order to do this, it's just a matter of counting up or down the scale. Here's a chart that will make this easier to do:

		Major			Minor	
Chords in C :	C	F	G7	Am	Dm	E7
Db:	Db	Gb	Ab7	Bbm	Ebm	F7
D:	D	G	A7	Bm	Em	F#7
Eb:	Eb	Ab	Bb7	Cm	Fm	G7
E :	E	A	B7	C#m	F#m	G#7
F :	F	Bb	C7	Dm	Gm	A7
Gb:	Gb	Cb	Db7	Ebm	Abm	Bb7
G:	G	C	D7	Em	Am	B7
Ab:	Ab	Db	Eb7	Fm	Bbm	C7
A :	A	D	E7	F#m	Bm	C#7
Bb:	Bb	Eb	F7	Gm	Cm	D7
B :	B	E	F#7	G#m	C#m	D#7

For example, if you wish to transpose a song in the key of C to the key of D, you would...

	The Original Chord		The New Chord
change	C	to	D
change	F	to	G
change	G7	to	A7
change	Am	to	Bm
change	Dm	to	Em
change	E7	to	F#7

In this case, everything moves up one whole step.

Notes On The Ukulele Fretboard

The Fretboard

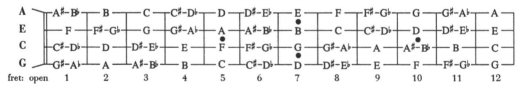

The Notes On Each String

The History Of The Ukulele

The story of the ukulele actually began in Portugal. In the summer of 1879, a boat arrived in Hawaii's Honolulu Harbor with 419 immigrants from the Portuguese island of Madeira. Upon arrival, one of the passengers, Joao Fernandez, began entertaining by-standers by playing a 4-string Portuguese instrument called a *braguinha*. In short order, the islanders became enchanted with the little instrument and promptly renamed it—ukulele. Pronounced *oo-koo-le-le* (and still to this day, pronounced this way in Hawaii), the name was Hawaiian for "jumping flea," which is exactly how the islanders described the effect of a player's fingers "jumping" around the fretboard.

Manuel Nuñes, another Madeiran, played a major role in transforming the braguin-ha into the modern day ukulele. Some of his refinements included replacing the steel strings with gut strings and altering the tuning slightly to allow for easier chord forma-tion. Along with some of the other great Hawaiian ukulele makers, Dias, and later, Santo, Kumalae and Kamaka, he discovered that the local koa tree produced a wood that was exceptionally light and resonant for uke manufacturing.

Hawaiian royalty also played a big part in the popularizing of the ukulele. King David Kalakaua, Queen Emma and the future Queen Liliuokalani (who later wrote the famous Hawaiian song "Aloha Oe") were all great ukulele admirers.

In 1915, Hawaii invested $100,000 in their Pavilion at the Panama-Pacific Exposition in San Francisco, and thousands of Americans heard the ukulele for the first time. In 1916, the Victor Record Company sold more Hawaiian records than any other style of music. U.S. guitar makers, sensing a new market, jumped in with their own uke designs. Companies like Martin, Gibson and National Resonator are three companies whose early ukes have become quite collectible. The '20s saw the emergence of two of the great uke players: both Roy Smeck and Cliff Edwards (Ukulele Ike) were considered "pop stars" of their time. Because of their efforts, much of the sheet music in the '20s and '30s featured ukulele chord diagrams.

Thanks to Arthur Godfrey, more waves of ukulele popularity occurred in the '40s—and in the '50s, as a result of the sale of millions of low-cost plastic ukuleles designed by Mario Maccaferri.

Now, there are only a handful of ukulele manufacturers (Kamaka is one of the few remaining Hawaiian makers). However, like you, there are still many avid ukulele fans. The annual Ukulele Festival in Hawaii continues to introduce new crops of children and teens to the joys of the uke. Japan, Canada and England are big uke markets, and in the mainland U.S., cities like Los Angeles can boast as many as three active ukulele clubs.

Alphabetical Song Contents

The author at work.
Photo by Elizabeth Maihock Beloff